MY SECRET

MY SECRET

ALSO BY FRANK WARREN

POSTSECRET

A POSTSECRET BOOK

MY SECRET

COMPILED BY FRANK WARREN

First published in hardback in Great Britain in 2007 by
Orion Books
an imprint of the Orion Publishing Group Ltd
Orion House, 5 Upper St Martin's Lane,
London WC2H 9EA
An Hachette Livre UK Company

3 5 7 9 10 8 6 4 2

A CIP catalogue record for this book is available
from the British Library.

ISBN: 978 0 7528 8987 0

Printed in Spain by Cayfosa-Quebecor

The Orion Publishing Group's policy is to use papers that are natural, renewable and recyclable and made from wood grown
in sustainable forests. The logging and manufacturing processes are expected to conform to the environmental regulations
of the country of origin.

Every effort has been made to fulfil requirements with regard to reproducing copyright material. The author and publisher will
be glad to rectify any omissions at the earliest opportunity.

www.orionbooks.co.uk

This book is dedicated to my daughter, and every other young person making that journey from the home they were born into toward the home they will create for themselves.

–Frank

FOREWORD

Frank Warren and the PostSecret community changed my life as founder of 1-800-SUICIDE.

In 1998, I founded the Kristin Brooks Hope Center and 1-800-SUICIDE in memory of my wife, Kristin, whom I lost to suicide triggered by postpartum depression following the stillbirth of our infant son. In January 2005, as we approached our two millionth call, all federal funds ended—seriously threatening the future of 1-800-SUICIDE. At a time when I finally had reason to hope I was making a difference, the threat of losing the hotline felt like I was losing Kristin again.

Earlier this year, Frank posted a plea for support on the PostSecret website. The outpouring from PostSecret readers was immediate and overwhelming. In just over one week, more than $30,000 was raised from over nine hundred contributors. Without the help of Frank and the PostSecret community, the nation would have lost an eight-year-old resource that has been connecting callers from fifty states to help and hope.

It has been a privilege to work with PostSecret and be a part of this healing process.

—Reese Butler

INTRODUCTION

In the past two years, I have received more than fifty thousand secrets mailed to me on artfully decorated postcards. Most secrets are sent anonymously, but the secrets that arrive from young people usually stand out; their passions run deeper, their loneliness feels more desolate, their joy is expansive. Their postcards reveal a hidden landscape and sound as though they come from brave explorers finding their way through a wilderness.

When I travel to college campuses and speak about the PostSecret Project with students, I have been inspired by the stories they have told me, stories that begin with a secret and end with hope. A young man in Seattle described how he gave his mother a copy of PostSecret as a gift, and how the secrets inside allowed them to discuss experiences and concerns they had never talked about before.

In Maryland, at the end of a talk, a courageous young woman stood up and showed all of us the T-shirt she designed that exposed the eating disorder she had hidden. On the front it read, *20% of all anorexics will die,* and on the back it listed the symptoms of the disease. "When I made my shirt and wore it to school, I was nervous to find out how my friends would react," she said, "but when my classmates saw it, they supported me and even asked me to make shirts like mine for them to wear too."

A woman in New York was emboldened to leave her abusive fiancé and remake her life after she recognized a secret she was keeping from herself on a stranger's postcard.

A teacher in Chicago told me that she displayed a "Veil of Secrets" at her school—a patchwork of more than three hundred postcards she collected from students. "It got students talking and caused people to feel more connected." She went on to tell me that it exasperated certain administrators, who removed it and declared, *What state standards could possibly support such gratuitous and sophomoric impulses?* (I went to high school in Illinois. I wish I had been lucky enough to have been in her class.)

Sometimes when I am on the road and feeling lost or lonely, I write a postcard home. Sharing my thoughts and feelings on a card usually helps me feel a little better. But what makes me feel more connected is imagining my card finding its way home and being placed in my mailbox by my favorite mail carrier. She groups the PostSecret cards into a stack a few inches high and then carefully secures the pile by wrapping two rubber bands around it, like a gift wrapped in a ribbon.

And that is how I imagine my postcard, bound together with everyone else's.

—Frank Warren

Post Secret
13345 Copper Ridge Rd.
German town, Maryland
20874-3454
USA

See me

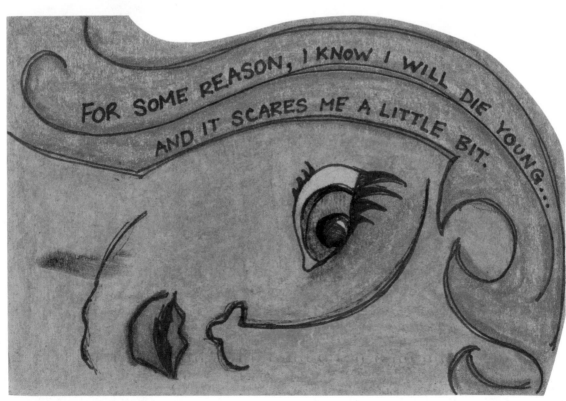

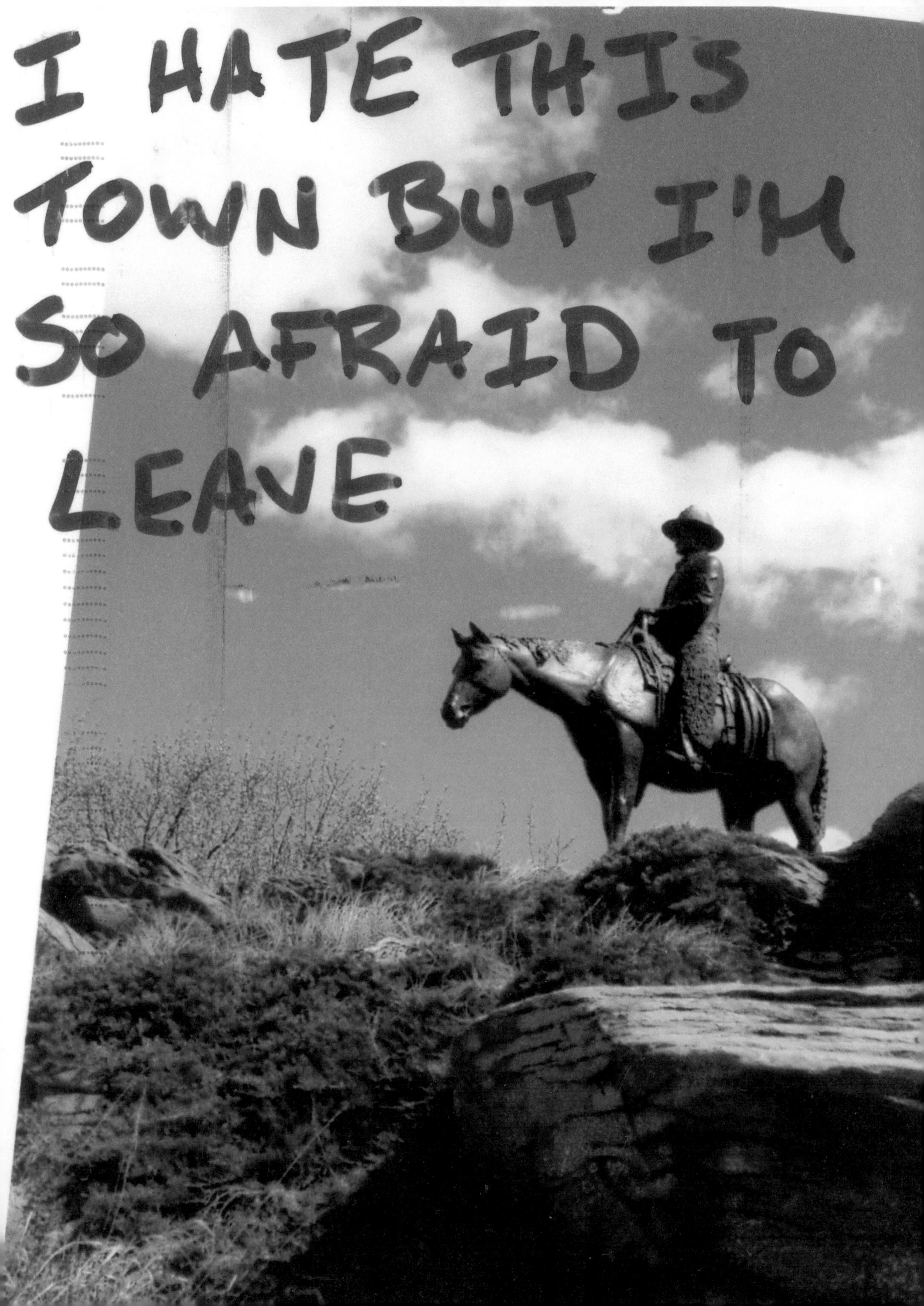
I HATE THIS TOWN BUT I'M SO AFRAID TO LEAVE

PostSecret
13345 Copper
Ridge Rd
Germantown MD
USA 20874-3454

GUTS LoVE MY
GUTS LoVE ME
THey LoVE US
FALLS

My Dreams are
Bigger
than this small
Apartment

I wish I had not tried to grow up so fast. I feel like I missed some important parts of young adulthood.

He left me any way.

i made deer hump.

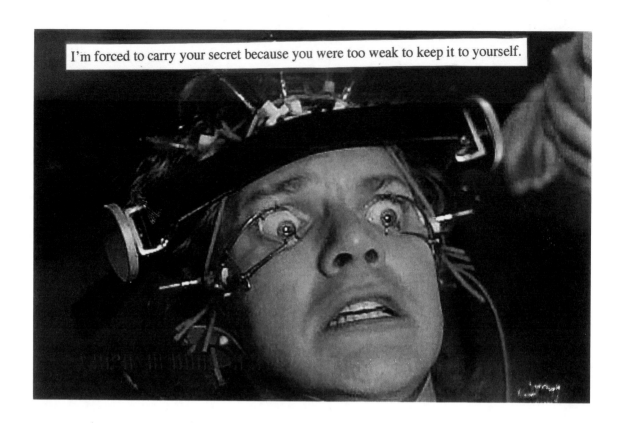

I'm forced to carry your secret because you were too weak to keep it to yourself.

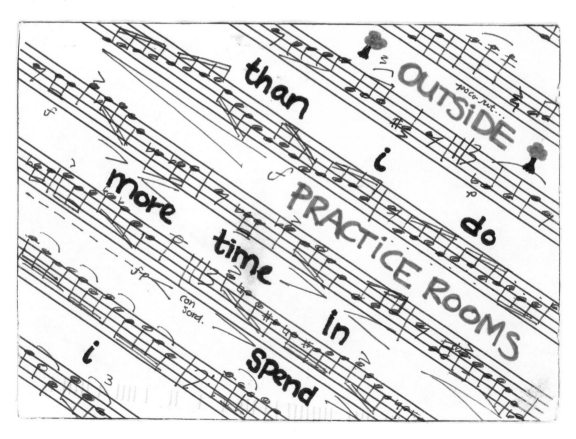

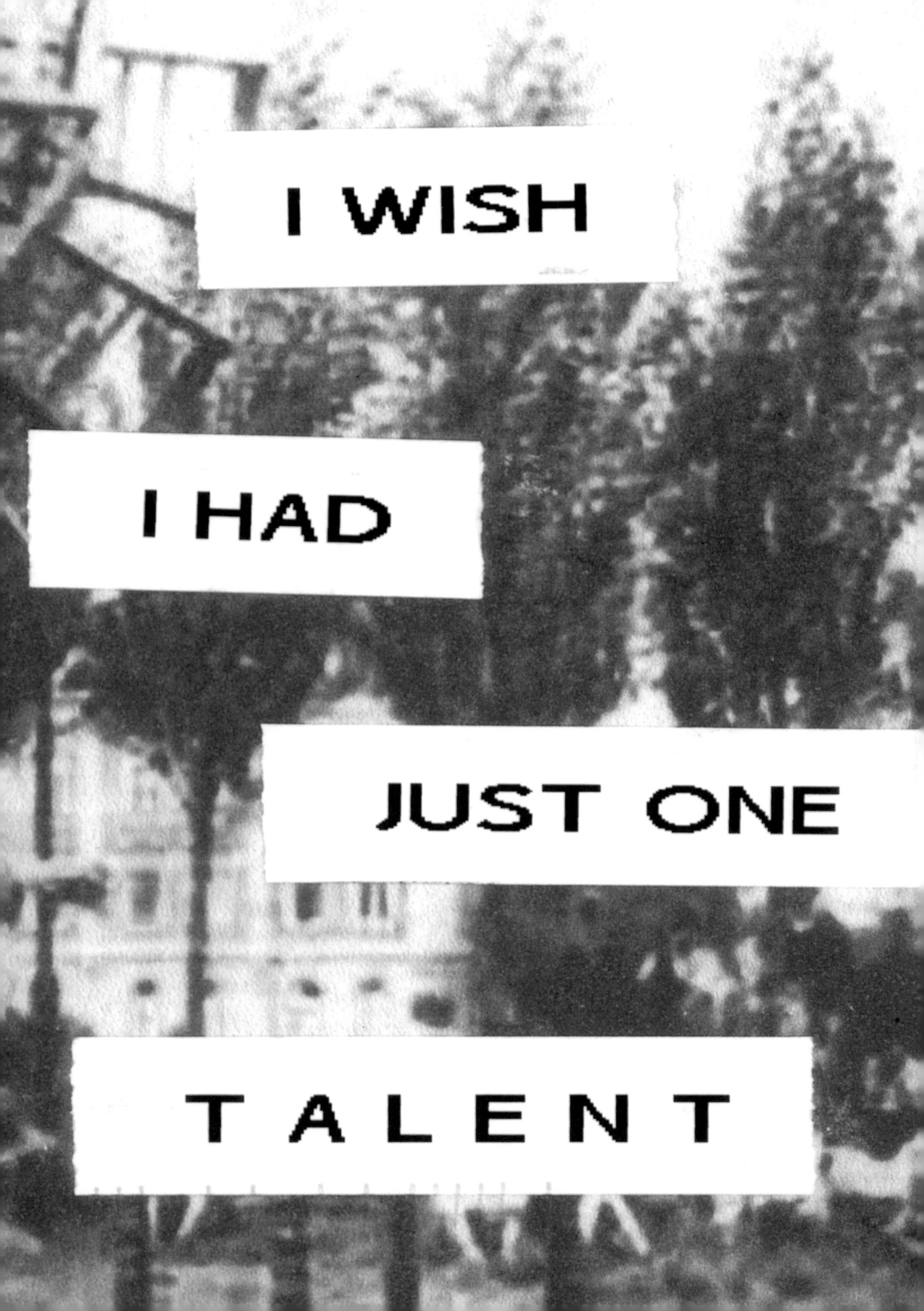

I WISH

I HAD

JUST ONE

TALENT

CHARGED BABY –

BABY

CHEAT BABY

BY THE

BITCH

screAm

BE R

AFT

THE PEOPLE

STI FOR

BE

H

In elementary school, I started lying and telling everybody I was allergic to peanuts. This is my first peanut butter cup in years. I had to eat it in my car so my fiance wouldn't see it. He thinks I'm allergic to them too.

sometimes i wish i didn't believe...

so i could stop feeling like i am just disappointing Him.

I drool,

a lot.

Although it's wonderful that you recommend 1(800) SUICIDE for suicidal people, not all people with secrets are depressed, oppressed, or scared. I think secrets are a good thing. It makes a person more mysterious, sexy, and unique. Secrets are fun, liberating; they make people who they are.

—Canada

I Lick the Inside
of Microwave Popcorn Bags

I showed a professor...

THE REAL ME!

I'M A Cheerleader;

but Secretly I deal drugs.

've watched my bipolar sister become a zombie on her meds.

I'm bipolar too

but I'm not seeking treatment

I like the highs and lows.....

i

 c u s s a t

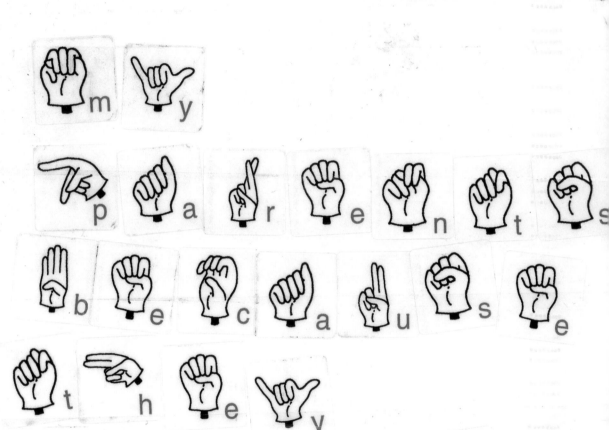 m y

p a r e n t s

b e c a u s e

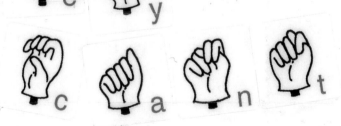 t h e y

c a n t

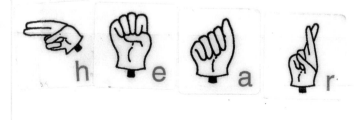 h e a r

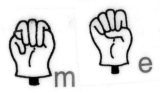 m e

! I was raped on a beach

I hate when ppl. talk about sex

on the beach as a sexy thing

I feel out of place in a group of friends

AND I'M frusturated with the fact that You <u>love</u> me? left Me Here.

I think I'd enjoy life on a deserted island because almost everybody gets on my nerves

Popular Meter
Queen
Bee
⊤—Me

I am avoiding you because you are socially below me.

You—⊥

Loser

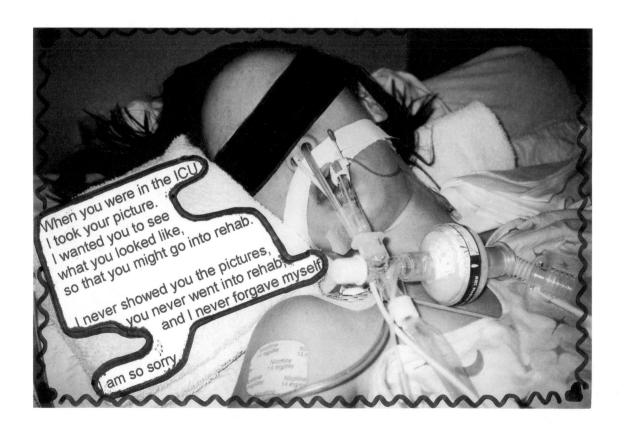

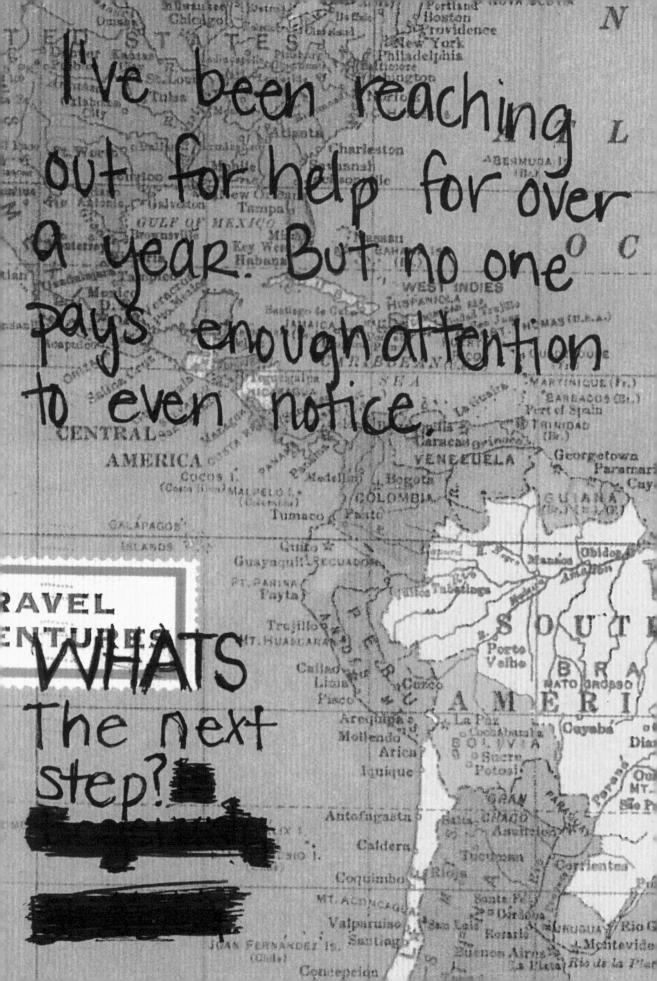

I've been reaching out for help for over a year. But no one pays enough attention to even notice.

WHATS The next step?

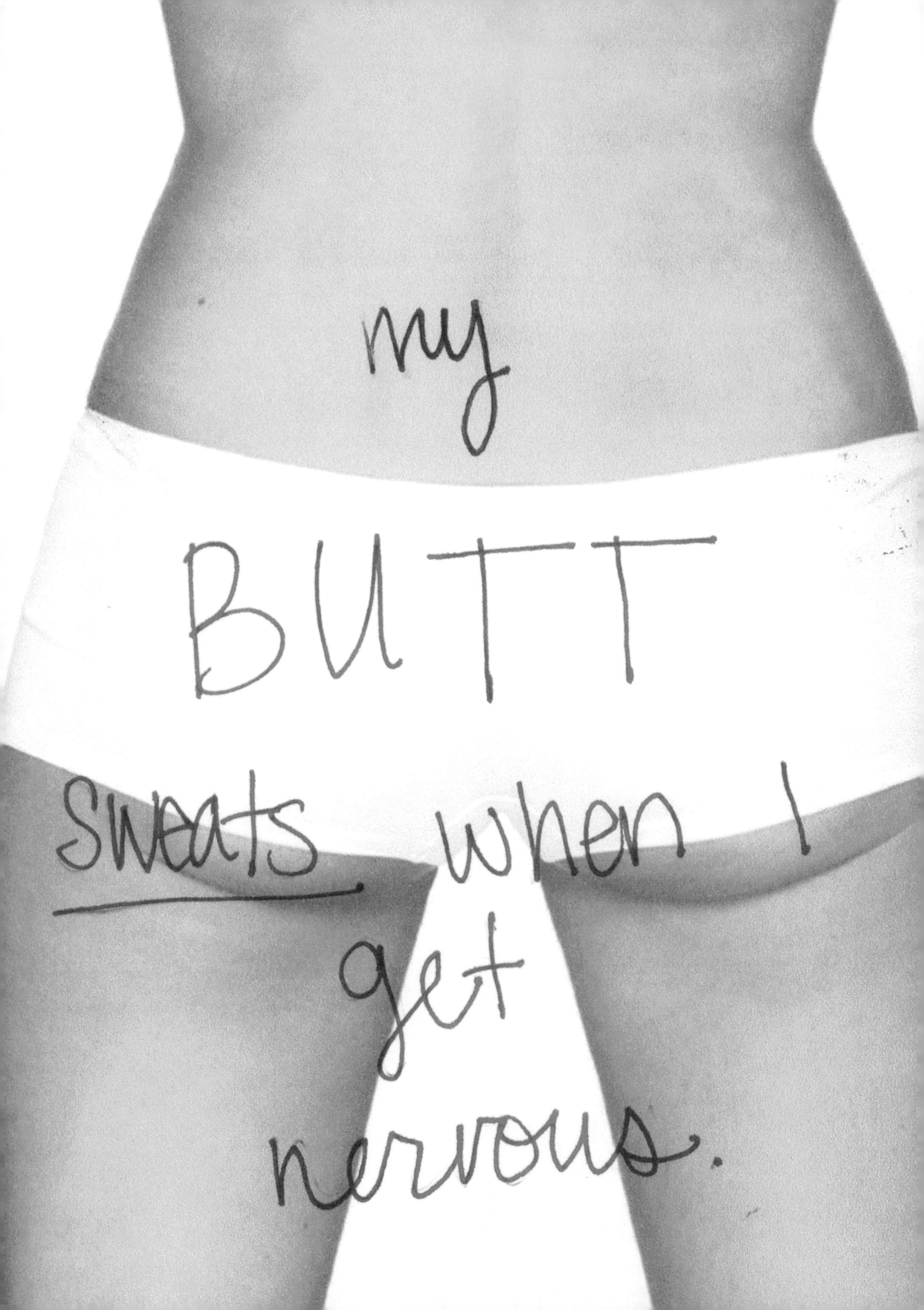

my

BUTT

sweats when I

get

nervous.

I have anger issues.

I know because

I often want

to kick the ass

of a total stranger

for no good reason.

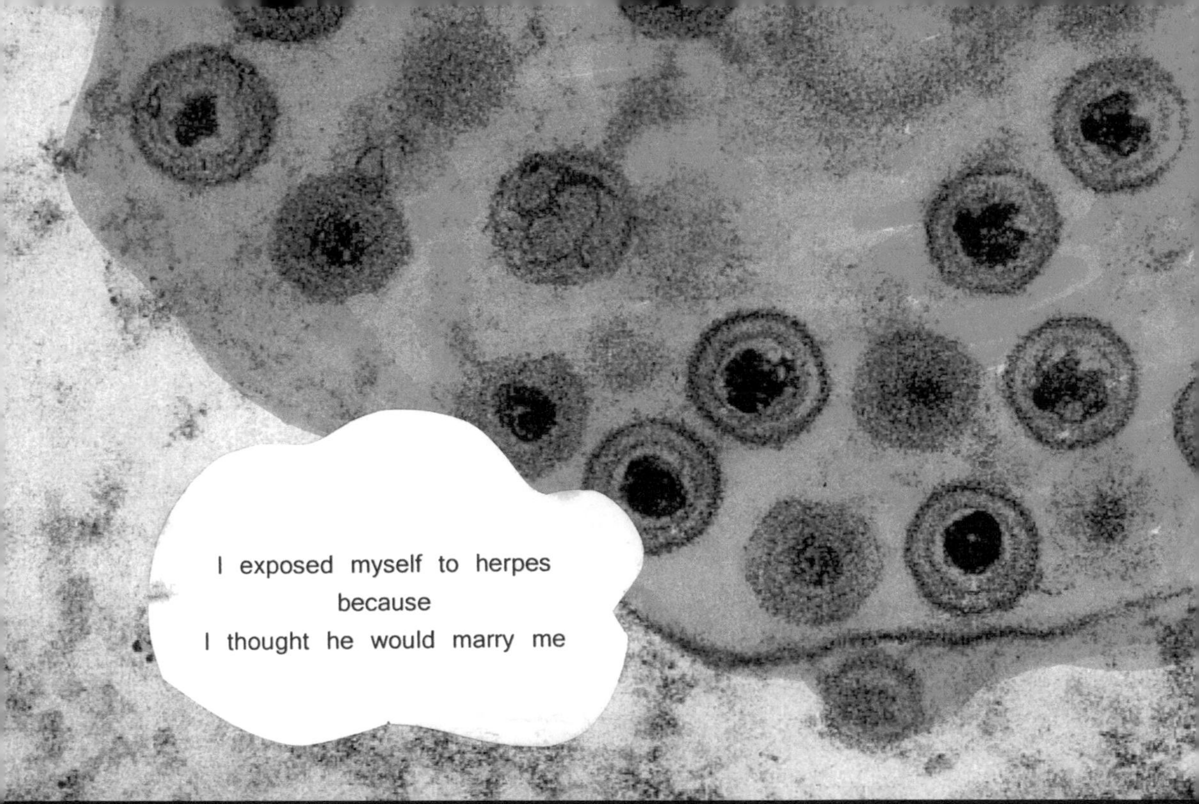
I exposed myself to herpes
because
I thought he would marry me

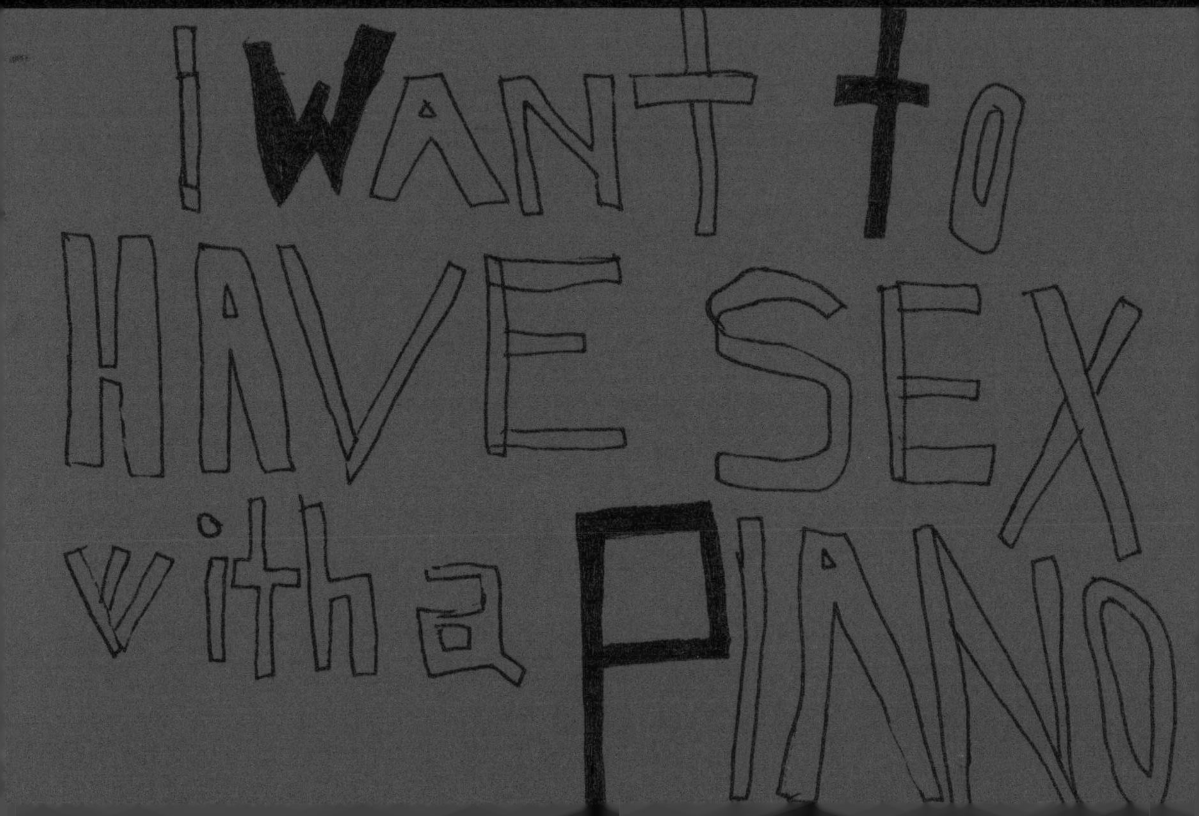
I WANT to
HAVE SEX
vith a PIANO

I don't feel entirely alone when I go through
still feel alone, but I feel like there are a lot

the postcards on your website, or rather, I
more people alone with me.

—New York

I call my friend really late at night, secretly hoping she'll fall asleep while we're on the phone. Sometimes she does, and then I lie down to sleep too.

I'm in love with her and I realize it's probably the closest I'll ever get to sleeping with her.

But for now, it's enough.

I faked my own...

GRADUATION

| 6 | 7 | 8 | 9 |

My mom puts a star on the calendar for every day I haven't cut myself.

| 13 | 14 | 15 | 16 |

I don't deserve 5 of those stars...

| 20 | 21 | 22 | 23 |

Sorry.

13 JUN 2005 PM 15 L

37 USA   37 USA

PostSecret
13345 Copper Ridge R
Germantown,
       Maryland
   20874-3454

20874-3454

everyday I worry
my exboyfriend
will use the naked
pictures I sent him
to ruin my life

I

TOLD

MYFAMILY

THESCHOOLNURSE

ANDMYOPTOMETRIST

THATICOULDNTSEETHELASTROWS

JUSTSOTHATIWOULDGETGLASSESLIKEMYFRIENDS

in the 3rd grade, a boy told me i looked like a werewolf because my arms were so hairy. for the rest of the year, i wore long-sleeved shirts and turtlenecks. even in the summer. now i just shave my arms.

i wonder if he remembers.

MY FAVOURITE PART ABOUT WORKING AT LEGO LAND IS DESTROYING ALL OF THE BUILDINGS THAT LITTLE KIDS CREATE

I have never been anyone's first choice.

Every regret I've ever had involved alcohol.

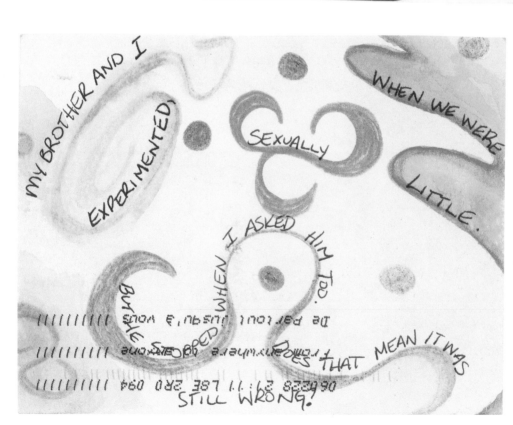

MY BROTHER AND I EXPERIMENTED, SEXUALLY WHEN WE WERE LITTLE. BUT SHE STOPPED WHEN I ASKED HIM TOO. DOES THAT MEAN IT WAS STILL WRONG?

I want to talk to somebody because they care

not because it's their job.

i know you didn't rape me

but i convinced myself that you did because i was unwilling to admit that i lost my virginity to you.

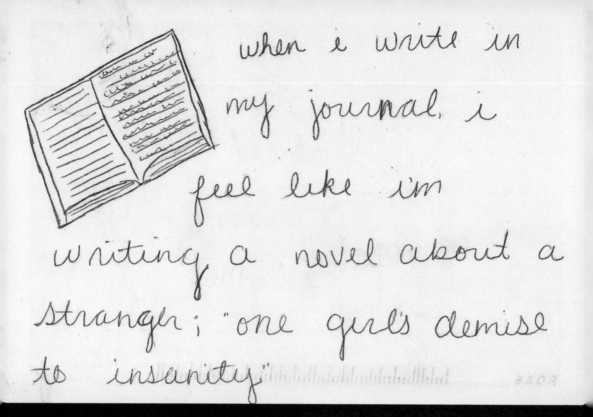

when i write in my journal, i feel like i'm writing a novel about a stranger; "one girl's demise to insanity"

HE SAID HE DIDN'T
LIKE CONDOMS
SO WE DIDN'T USE ONE...
BUT I DIDN'T TELL HIM
I HAVE HERPES.....

POSTSECRET
13345 COPPER RIDGE RD
GERMANTOWN, MARYLAND
20874-3454

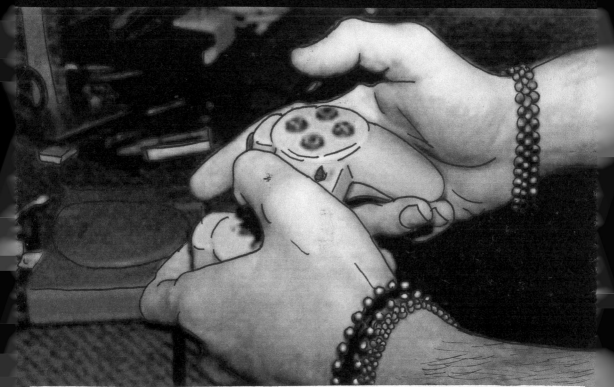

Barely Here.

I'm extra nice to blacks to show them that I am nothing like my forefathers.

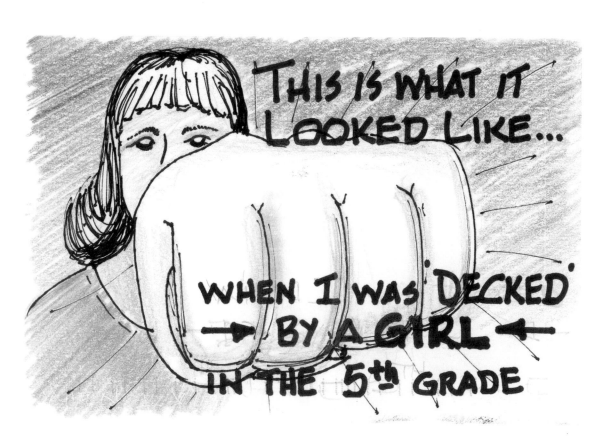

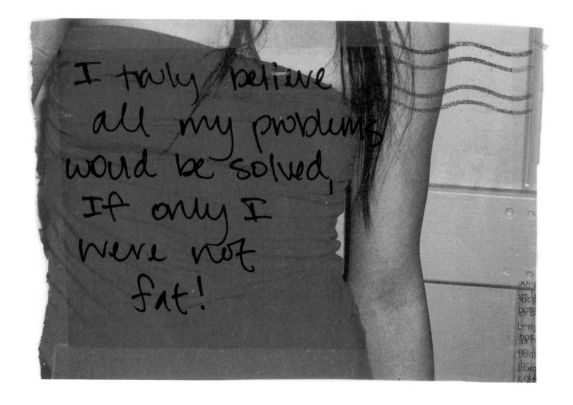

for so long

to be me

I can't wait till I prove them all wrong.

this was supposed to help me feel less anxious and sad.

now I feel nothing at all.

I Can't Stand my Roommate.

I cheated my way through

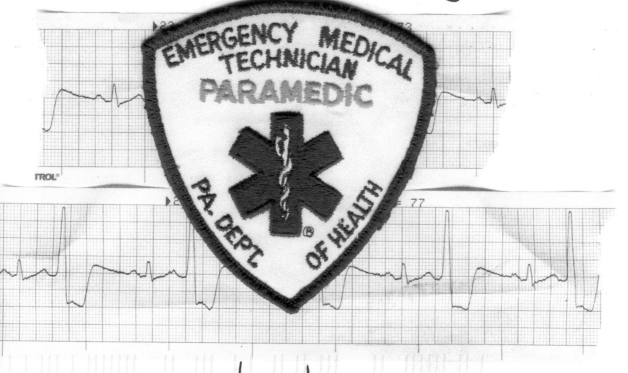

school.

Marc
Caitlin
Lana

Carr
Lauren
hae
niel

I still look at your 3rd grade picture and think what might have happened...

Laura
Ben
Megan

Stephanie
Taylor
Emily

Adrier
Natali
Nick
Tabit!

**If I hadn't moved
825 miles away**

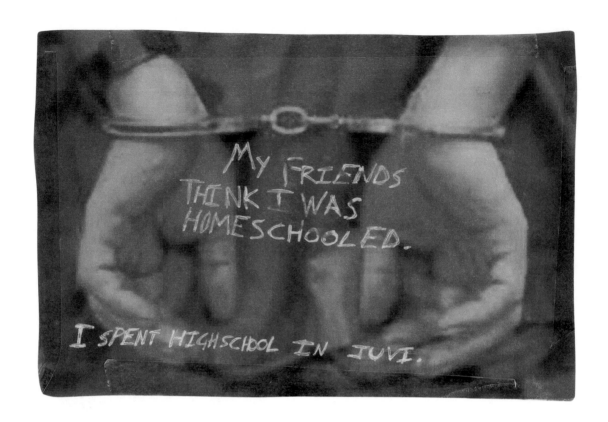

MY FRIENDS
THINK I WAS
HOMESCHOOLED.

I SPENT HIGHSCHOOL IN JUVI.

THE CATCHER
IN THE RYE

J. D. SA

If you feel like you are going insane
and you are trapped in a
dysfunctional environment,
You Are Not Crazy.

- POST SECRET -
13345 CopperRidge Rd.
GERMANTOWN, MD.
20874

EVERYTIME I'M ON THE PHONE TO MY PARENTS I HAVE.. TO POOP.

For Better

He tries to make me happy • He likes to keep the apartment clean • He's great in bed--we really have great sex together • I love it when we cuddle • He teases me in a fun way • I like waking up next to him • I enjoy feeling him inside me • His happiness makes me happy • He doesn't like me to swear or yell at him • He helps me avoid mistakes • He says I turn him on • I like to think of ways to make him happier • My family likes him a lot and thinks he is good person for me to be with • He asked me if I want to get married

For Worse

He frustrates me • I do most of the cleaning while he relaxes • He's not interested in sex most of the time • He develops various pains when we cuddle • I can't tease back • He's very grumpy when he wakes up • He'd rather jack-off • He is easily offended or angered • He swears and yells at me • He critiques almost everything I do • Other people turn him on a lot more • He doesn't think of me most of the time • I don't tell them any of this because I don't want them to think negatively of him • I'm not sure if I do, but I said yes.

I sleep to escape

My grandmother used to mail me postcards (like this) (blank ones) so I would write to her. She died seven years ago, and I just found this one in the attic. I'm sorry Grandma.

I should have written more

Sometimes I
WiSH

I was better
at faking
it.

Sometimes when we think we are keeping

a secret, that secret is actually keeping us.

—Frank

Inside this envelope are the scraps of my old life.

But I realized... I don't need this anymore. I'm alive again. Everything is okay. My soul has been reborn! I couldn't be more happy!

And let me tell you.....

there is nothing more invigorating or life-affirming then shredding old suicide notes.

fuck the odds.

I SAW YOUR SECRET...

POSTAGE DUE ___2___

POST SECRET
13345 COPPER RIDGE RD
GERMANTOWN, MARYLAND
20874

R046   AND I LOVE YOU ANYWAY.

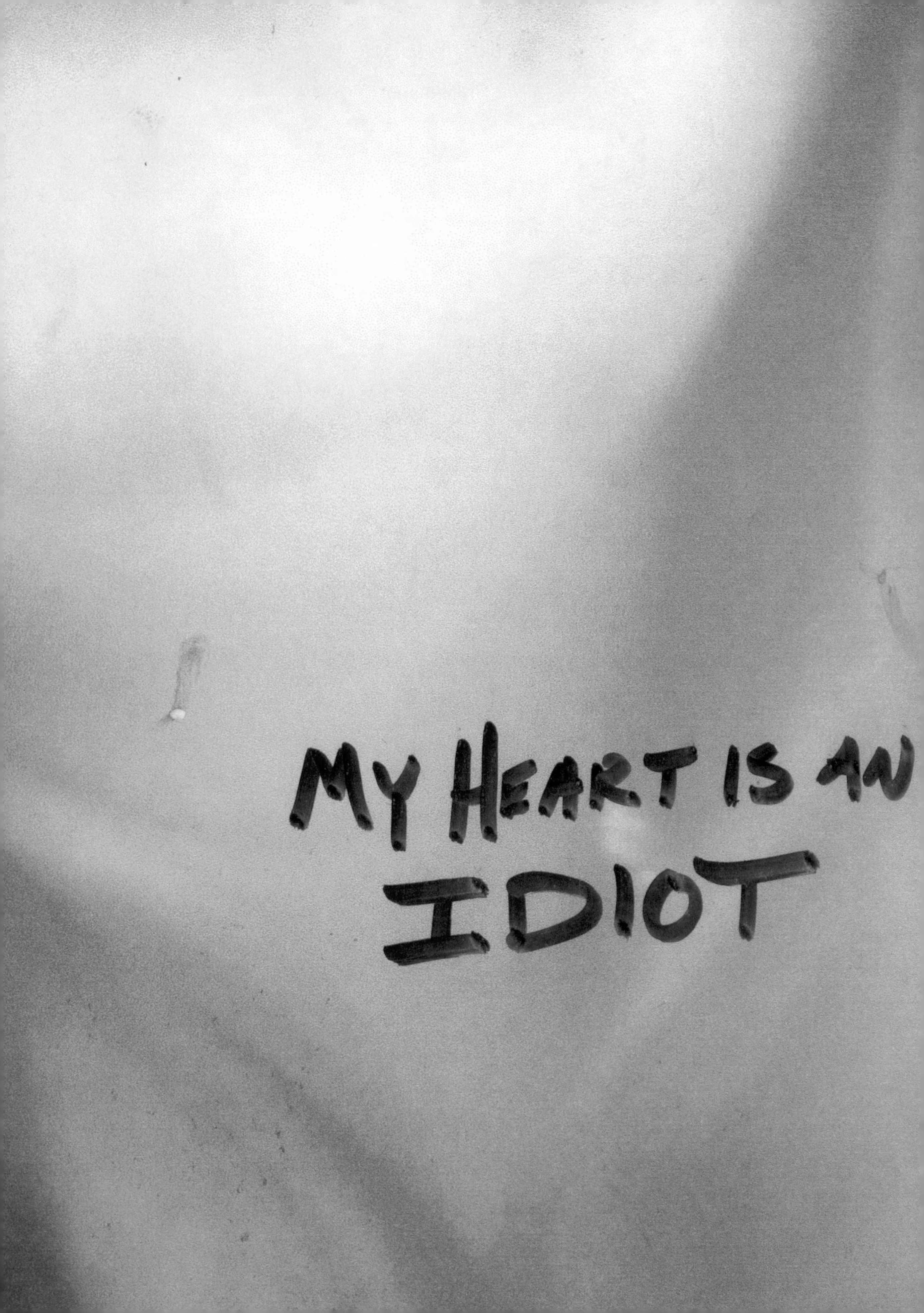
MY HEART IS AN
IDIOT

I Am Afraid That the only Thing I like to Do, Won't TAKE me anywhere.

I hope I am wrong.

sometimes...

i miss God.

I was molested for most of my childhood.

Sometimes I liked it.

I will always hate myself for that.

If I died no one would notice.

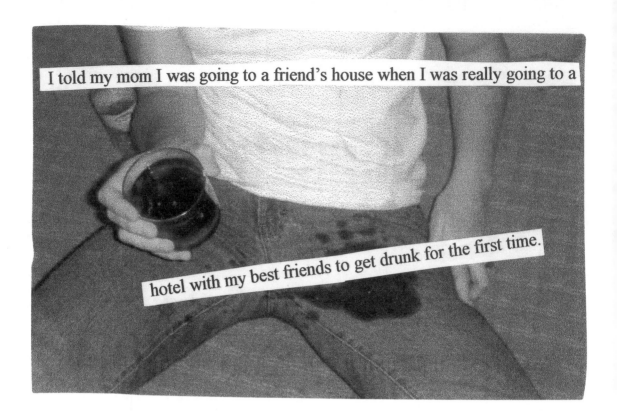

I told my mom I was going to a friend's house when I was really going to a hotel with my best friends to get drunk for the first time.

I hate highschool because it has made my best relationships go up in smoke.

I am afraid to live
a Christian life
because I might
miss out
on all the fun

When do we tell them

there will be TWO brides on the cake?

When I masturbate, the first thought that pops into my head after I climax is
"OK, what was the point of that?"

I lie to my mother about my finances so she won't worry about me. She thinks my bills are paid. In reality I am in debt $85000.

You think I don't but

I know

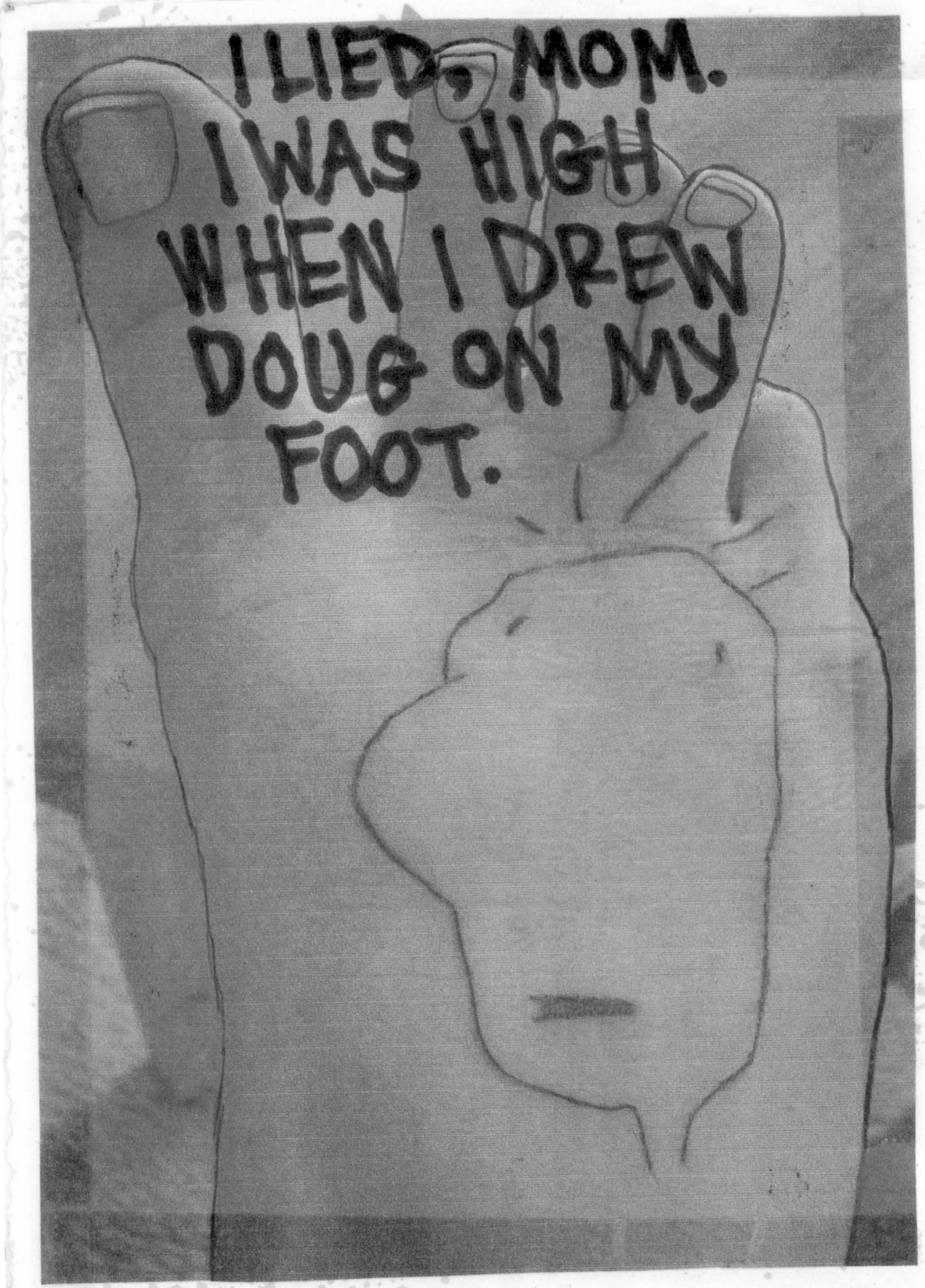
I LIED, MOM.
I WAS HIGH
WHEN I DREW
DOUG ON MY
FOOT.

I will always be the weird quiet girl.

It's always been my dream to attend Harvard Law School.

Now that I'm here, I'm counting down the days until I can leave

Then I remembered myself.

Enjoy your new important life and f*@k you.

You were the only one I thought I could count on.

(I was molested)

Then I said it

I desperately want someone
to recognize one of my
secrets so I can finally
stop pretending

What YOU!
did will not
Define ME!
I Broke FREE!

I work with a lot of old people and they drive me nuts

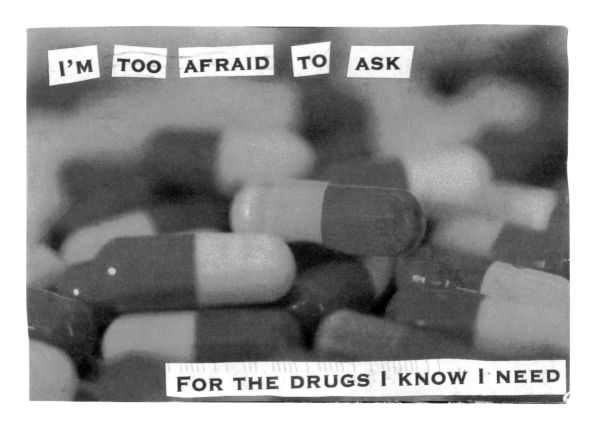

I'M TOO AFRAID TO ASK

FOR THE DRUGS I KNOW I NEED

I don't remember when jumping on the bed stopped being fun... but I dream of returning to such carefree days...

I WAS A BITCH TO YOU

I KNEW YOU LOVED ME

I'M SO SORRY

I don't believe that "perfect families" exist...
They all fuck you up...

i sometimes wish no one told me i was adopted

Even though it will ruin all of my future plans, I am trying to get pregnant so that he can't leave me.

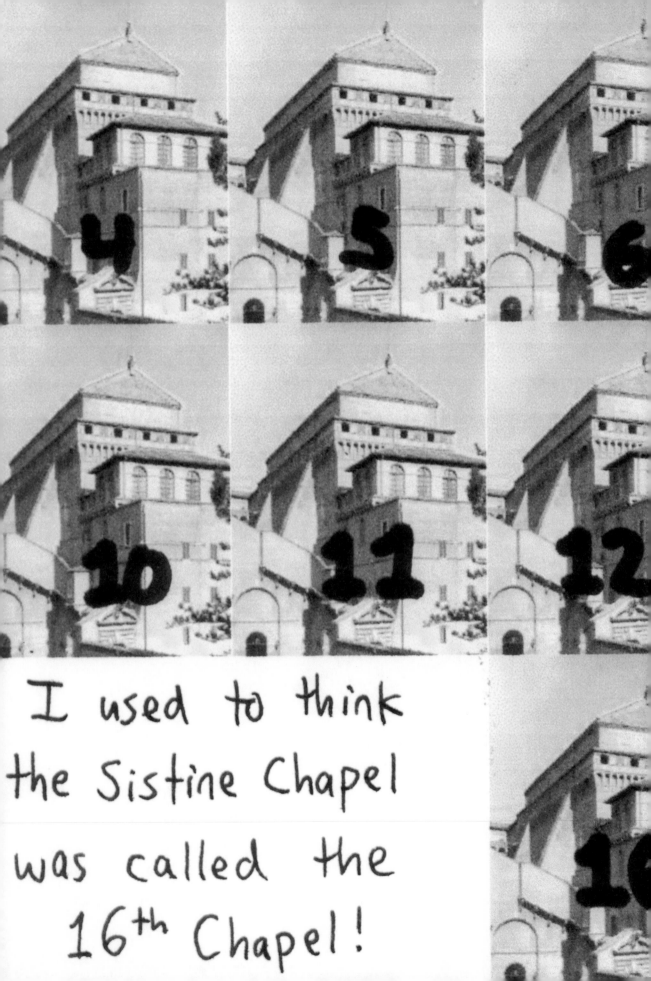

I used to think the Sistine Chapel was called the 16th Chapel!

My parents found out I am gay. They hate gays. They are disgusted by me. I tell myself that I hate them for rejecting me. I would do anything, any sick, immoral, Godless thing to hear them say

I love you No matter what.

I SEE YOU SEE ME.

ASK ME.
I'LL SAY
YES.

I lied to everyone to fit in and now feel more alone then ever before.

I'm not sure how I'm going to do this for the rest of my life.

Anorexia ate my SOUL

I'm not as smart as I lead on.

REVEAL

THIS IS ME BEFORE I REACH THE POINT OF NO RETURN.

I don't know how to say

NO

I am terrified of growing up.

In 6th grade I read something about, father's molesting their daughters.

So, I stopped hugging my dad for over a year.

I love my father.

I can't imagine how much I hurt him.

The first time I had an orgasm during intercourse I was 24!

He was my 11th lover and we'd already been intimate for over 9 months

I'd thought I was broken

Post Secret
13345 Copper Ridge
Germantown, MD
20874-3454

I CUT MY HAIR OFF CUS MY PARENTS love their SALON more THAN ME

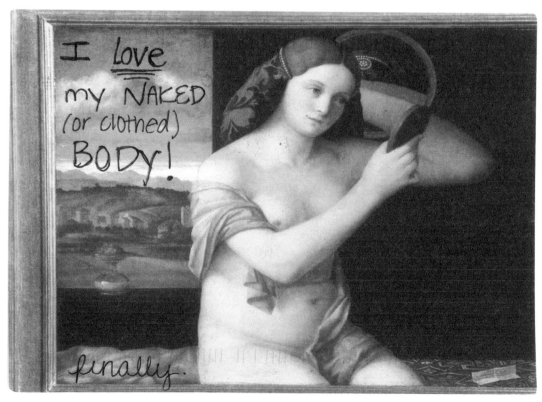

SHE SHOWED ME HERS
&
I SHOWED HER MINE

I'm starting to realize that all my problems can't be blamed on anything else but myself – only I can make my life what I want it to be and everyday my self-control and self-discipline fuck it up more and more.

I miss the days when I thought there was something wrong with me.

I'M SORRY MOM,
I'M SPENDING YOUR
MONEY ON THINGS
THAT ARE KILLING ME

I am afraid that since my Dad is GAY that I might be too.

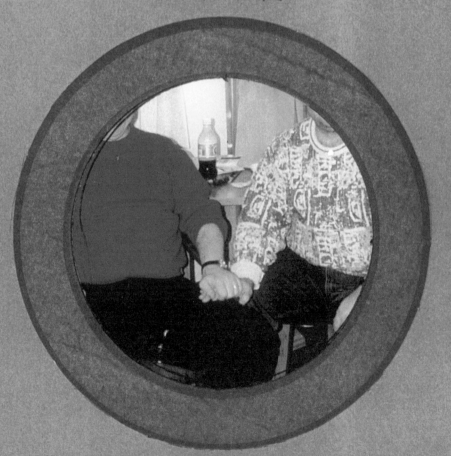

if i had a time machine, i would not kill hitler
or meet jesus

i would take you to the movies.

I got my nipple pierced.

I'm only 16.

And my mom doesnt know.

(it looks better than
this guy's)

I finally found my way.

SURPRISE!

ADOLECENCE IS NOT AN EXITING ADVENTURE

IT'S ACTUALLY VERY BORING

AND LONLIER THAN YOU COULD EVER IMAGINE.

I haven't told you everything.

The dog NEVER ate my home work

DISPOSABLE CAMERAS $10

2004 ~~WARPED~~ COMP 52 BANDS $5

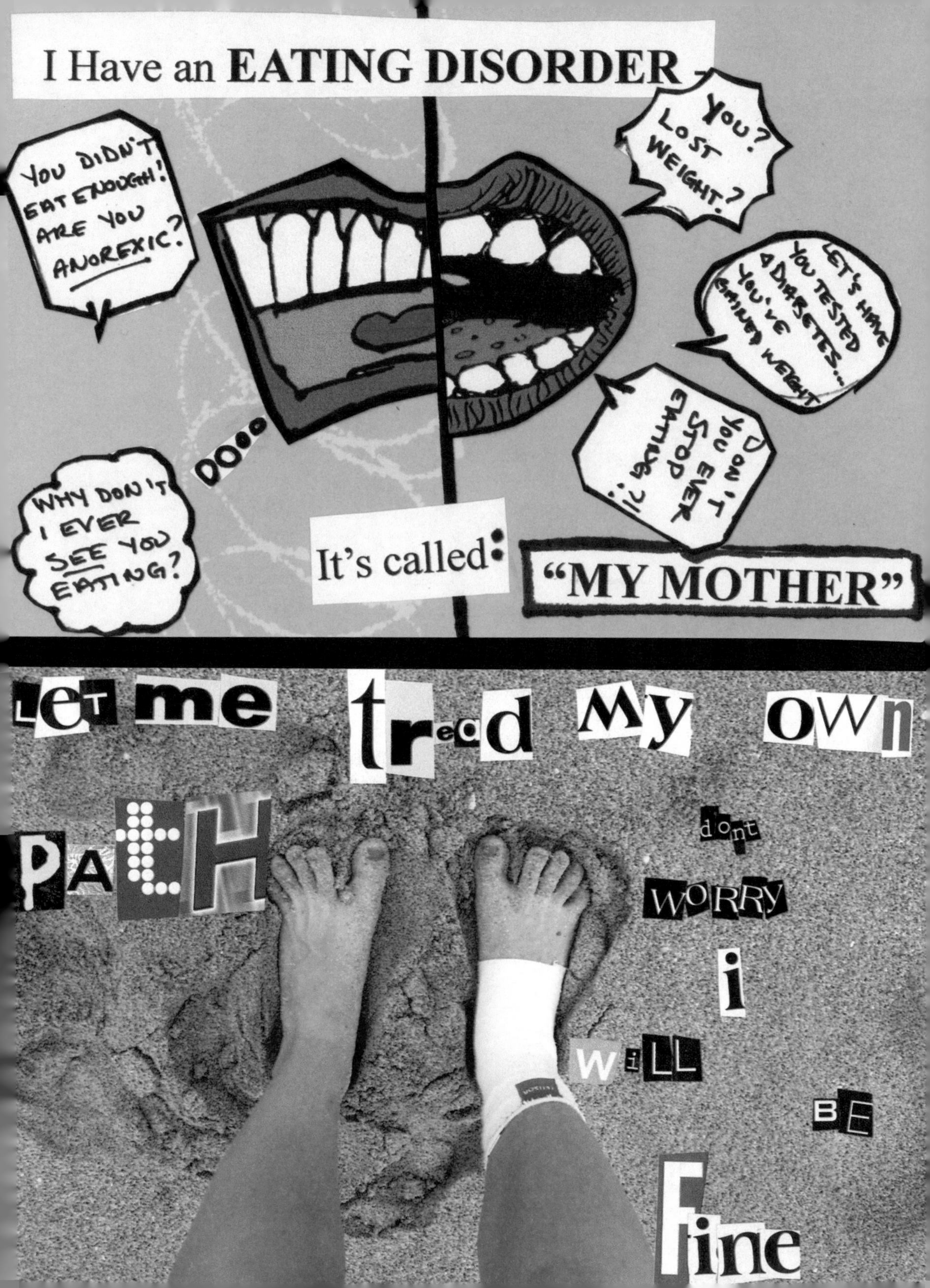
I Have an EATING DISORDER
YOU DIDN'T EAT ENOUGH! ARE YOU ANOREXIC?
YOU? LOST WEIGHT?
LET'S HAVE YOU TESTED 4 DIABETES... YOU'VE GAINED WEIGHT
DON'T YOU EVER STOP EATING?!
DOoo
WHY DON'T I EVER SEE YOU EATING?
It's called:
"MY MOTHER"
let me tread my own path
dont worry
i will be fine

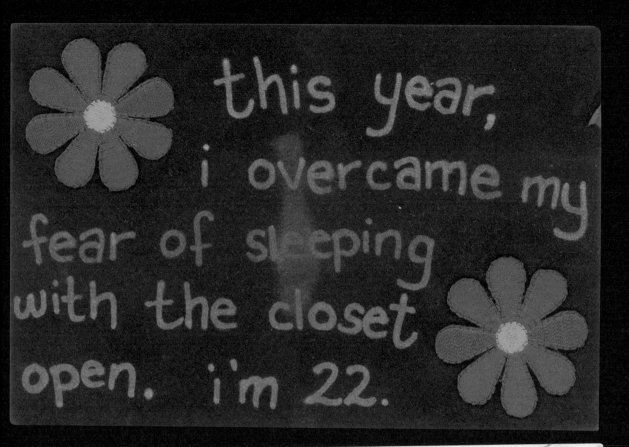

this year, i overcame my fear of sleeping with the closet open. i'm 22.

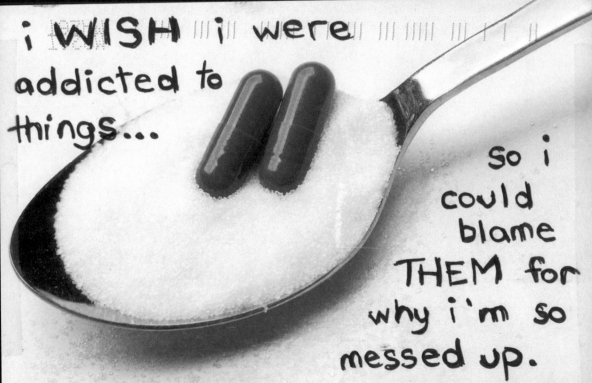

i WISH i were addicted to things...

so i could blame THEM for why i'm so messed up.

i kept the letter your boyfriend wrote for you and put it in my room so someone might find it and think that someone is in love with me....

I miss you
I love you
but I dont know who you are

YET

Maybe this isn't what she/he wants or immediately wanted to say what I told myself School doesn't last forever . . . it will not

needs to hear, but when I read the card I
for those four years: It's going to be okay.
define your life.

—Japan

I can't pee with someone next to me...

I fear someone will see my small penis

I'm afraid that deep down I am truly unworthy of another person's love.

I'm scared to tell you that I'm scared. Are you scared too?

People don't change...
They just find new ways
to lie to you...

As a little Girl I Dreamed of flying one of these.

Now I just flirt with men in the military cause they have the future my parents would never let me have

← F-18

I accidentally stumbled across my dad's porn stash....

And it turns out that he has a fetish.

this
will give me nightmares
for a
week

If my dad would have talked to
me about sex, would I have still

I wiSh Death

Chemistry

upon my teachers

I know I have a secret inside me,
but I don't know what it is.

I've realized that the most thrilling stories I have to tell people are about all the times I spent at the local park with my two best friends.

(and I'm really <u>okay</u> with that.)

When I was fourteen I tried to commit suicide with a razor, then with pills. Now that I am thirty I understand that my teenage problems were resolvable. I would have missed out on things like being a parent, my nephews, getting my first tattoo, learning to ride a motorcycle and falling in love. Even though I will have these scars on my arms for life I am glad I didn't die.

When I was a kid I thought I was Special

Now I'm not so sure

I

anonymously

mail

e.e. cummings

poems

to people

dream i had once i was away up in the sky Blue,everything:
was made of brass hangIng from strings (or)someThing i was
bar it was cOOl i didn't have anything on and I was hot all
bar was

there's just room for me in You
goes into your Little Stomach My legs are in your legs Your

me around; my head fits(my head)in your Brain—my,head's
thing

)with your head.all big

I Once
wrote a poem
about you on a $1
bill in hopes that one day
it will end up in your wallet ....

I recorded my cat meowing on a minicassette and hid it in the school library on "play".

I steal photographs from my Grandma.
...Because I find it hard to see things from her point of view

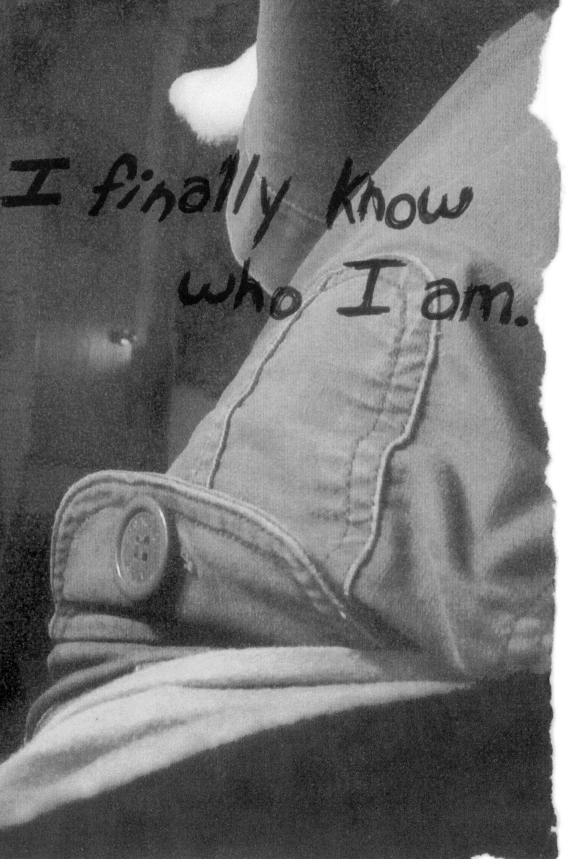

I just finished up seven years working at a mail center, and over that time I would come across PostSecret postcards, and take the time to read them. Some were funny, some touching, some heartbreaking. But every time I read them I knew I was in a privileged position—not only because I was perhaps one of the first people to read these beautifully crafted cards, but also because I was being let into somebody's soul and sharing with them whatever emotion they invested into creating the card.

I just want to let people out there know that even if your postcard doesn't show up on the website, there's a hardworking postal worker who is taking the time to read your secret, and who identifies with this brave, faceless, nameless sender.

—New Zealand

FRANK WARREN is a small business owner who started PostSecret as a community art project. Since October 2004, Warren has received thousands of anonymous postcards, which have been featured in galleries, a traveling art exhibit, the popular music video for the All-American Rejects' "Dirty Little Secret," and, most recently, in the bestselling book *PostSecret*. Ranked by *New York* magazine as the third most popular blog on the Internet, Warren's website earned several awards at both the 2006 Bloggy and Webby Awards and continues to attract over 3 million visitors a month. Warren has appeared on *Today, 20/20*, CNN, MSNBC, NPR, and Fox News, among others. Warren lives in Germantown, Maryland, with his wife and daughter.

www.postsecret.com